T0022595

NATURE'S GOT TALENT

SUPERSTAR FISH

Louise Spilsbury

PowerKiDS
press.

New York

Published in 2015 by The Rosen Publishing Group
29 East 21st Street, New York, NY 10010

Copyright © 2015 by The Rosen Publishing Group

All rights reserved. No part of this book may be reproduced in any form
without permission in writing from the publisher, except by a reviewer.

Produced for Rosen by Calcium Creative Ltd
Editor for Calcium Creative Ltd: Sarah Eason
US Editor: Joshua Shadowens
Designer: Paul Myerscough

Photo credits: Cover: Shutterstock: C Delacy (right), Eric Isselee (left), Stockpix4u (top).
Inside: Corbis: Billy Hustace 24; Dreamstime: Alessandrozocc 5b, Allnaturalbeth 17t, Lukas
Blazek 1, 25t, Alexandru-radu Borzea 9t, Briankieft 8, Katrina Brown 9b, Carol Buchanan
13t, Bugtiger 11t, Richard Carey 19t, Luis Fernando Chavier 12–13, Chuyu 11b, Tom
Dowd 20, Goruppa 10, Marc Henauer 6, Johannesk 2–3, 19b, Jtafalla1961 17b,
Kelpfish 7b, Kornilovdream 4, Lunamarina 21b, Mastervasyl 21t, Steven Melanson 15b,
Krzysztof Odziomek 5t, Puddingpie 7t, Jordan Tan 28, Tim Heusinger Von Waldegge 15t;
Shutterstock: A Cotton Photo 16, Rich Carey 27t, Nantawat Chotsuwan 18, Bill Kennedy
14, 29b, Stephan Kerkhofs 22, MP cz 25b, Anna Segeren 13b, 29t, Sergio Maldonado
Gts 27b, Totophotos 26, Kristina Vackova 23t, Richard Whitcombe 23b.

Library of Congress Cataloging-in-Publication Data

Spilsbury, Louise, author.
Superstar fish / by Louise Spilsbury.
    pages cm. — (Nature's got talent)
Includes index.
ISBN 978-1-4777-7068-9 (library binding) — ISBN 978-1-4777-7069-6 (pbk.) —
ISBN 978-1-4777-7070-2 (6-pack)
1. Fishes—Juvenile literature. I. Title.
QL617.2.S65 2015
597—dc23
                                                                  2014001264

Manufactured in the United States of America

CPSIA Compliance Information: Batch #WS14PK7: For Further Information contact Rosen Publishing, New York, New York at 1-800-237-9932

Contents

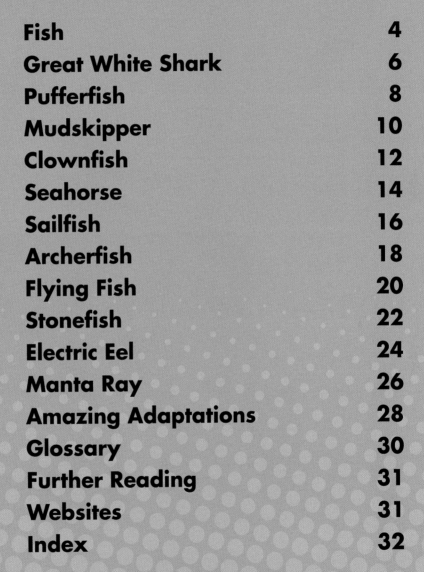

Fish

There are more than 30,000 types of fish in the world, and they are all fantastic in their own way. Fish come in a huge range of shapes and sizes. Some are big and round, others are as flat as a frisbee. There are many different types of fantastic fish but all fish have some things in common.

Fish have fins that help them move through water. Most fish are also covered in **scales**.

All fish are **vertebrates**. They have a backbone, or spine, and a skeleton in their bodies.

All fish live in water and have special body parts called **gills** that allow them to breathe.

Fish Superstars

All fish are amazing, but some are more astonishing than others! In this book we are going to find out about some of the world's most talented fish superstars.

The whale shark is the largest fish in the world. It looks like a whale but it lays eggs like other fish.

Secret Stars

The coelacanth is sometimes called a living **fossil**. Until 1938, when the first live coelacanth was discovered, only fossils of the fish had been found and people believed it was extinct. This fish swam in the oceans in prehistoric times.

Great White Shark

The powerful body of the great white shark is streamlined so it can swim in short, fast bursts.

The great white shark is the ultimate killing machine. Growing up to 20 feet (6.1 m) long, this impressive beast is also the biggest fish **predator** on Earth. Once the creature has **prey** in its sights, there is little chance of escape. The torpedo-shaped giant uses its powerful tail to speed through the water at up to 15 miles (24 km) per hour in pursuit of its meal.

The great white shark is named for its white belly.

Stealth Attack

The great white shark has a white belly but a gray back so when sea lions, seals, and other prey animals look down into deep water they cannot easily see the shark. This allows it to sneak up on prey. When the shark is directly below prey, it shoots up from the deep and slams into its victim, which usually knocks it out.

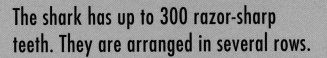

The shark has up to 300 razor-sharp teeth. They are arranged in several rows.

Top Talent

The great white shark has superb hearing and eyesight. It also has an amazing sense of smell. This acute sense of smell allows the shark to find weak and injured prey from a great distance. A great white shark can smell blood in the water up to 3 miles (5 km) away!

Pufferfish

Pufferfish look like ordinary fish until threatened. Then, these curious creatures speedily puff themselves up until they are several times their normal size. They look like large, spiky beach balls! At this size, the fish are almost impossible for a predator to eat.

The pufferfish can swallow large amounts of water and air to inflate itself quickly.

The pufferfish has a very flexible stomach that can expand in size quickly and easily.

Most pufferfish also have spines on their skin, which protrude only when the fish are inflated.

A Deadly Dinner

Any predator that does manage to eat a pufferfish soon regrets it! There are around 120 different types of pufferfish. Many of them contain a deadly poison that tastes terrible and kills other fish. In fact, there is enough **toxin** in just one pufferfish to kill 30 adult humans.

Some pufferfish have colorful markings to warn animals they are poisonous. Others blend in with their background.

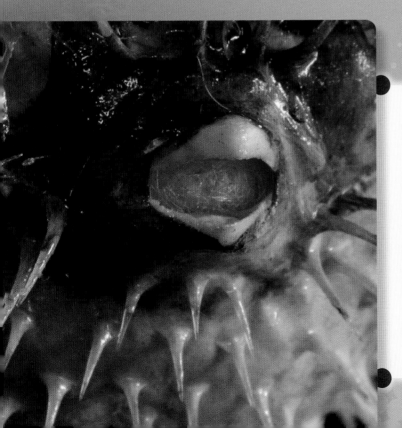

Top Talent

Pufferfish have four large teeth that are fused together to form a hard beak. Some types of pufferfish use their beaks to scrape algae from rocks to eat. Other pufferfish use their beaks to break open clams, mussels, and other shellfish to eat.

Mudskipper

Mudskippers are amazing fish that can walk on land. They live in swamps and estuaries and scuttle back and forth between the water and the mud flats. Not only can these comical creatures swim, they can walk, jump, and climb, too. Before climbing onto land, the fish fill their gills with water, to create an **oxygen** tank that allows them to breathe on land.

The mudskipper uses its muscular tail to jerk forward on its fins.

The mudskipper's muscular side fins are placed under its body to enable the fish to walk on them.

10

Up Periscope!

When swimming or walking in shallow, muddy water, the fish can move its eyes up and down and in and out of the water, just like a submarine periscope. The mudskipper can also move its eyes to look in different directions. This allows the fish to see in every direction when it is swimming with its head above water.

The mudskipper uses its eyes to look out for danger in any direction.

Secret Stars

This big, bad, and ugly fish has sometimes been named Fishzilla! The curious northern snakehead fish has a mean set of teeth and delivers a vicious bite. It also has the ability to breathe air and wriggle for short distances across land. It has even been seen in backyard ponds!

Clownfish

The clownfish is named for its clown-like colors, but this creature is no fool! It is a super-smart con artist that lives among the poisonous tentacles of sea anemones, without ever being stung. The fish's skin is covered in mucus that fools the anemone into believing the fish is just another part of itself. The fish hides from predators among the anemone's tentacles.

The clownfish rarely moves more than 12 inches (30 cm) from the protection of its anemone.

The clownfish lives alone, in pairs, or in small groups. It attacks predators that come near its anemone by chasing and biting them, or beating them with its tail.

Top Talent

The black stripes between the orange and white colors of a clownfish are different widths on different types of the fish. Clownfish that live within large sea anemones have thick, black stripes. The stripes help to **camouflage** the clownfish among the shadows of the anemone's moving tentacles.

A Perfect Partnership

Sea anemones provide clownfish with food as well as protection. The clownfish eat the remains of any fish meals not finished by the anemone. In return, the clownfish keeps the anemone healthy by eating its rotten or damaged tentacles, as well as many small **invertebrates** that damage the anemone.

The clownfish swims among a sea anemone's tentacles, safe from predators that dare not get too close to the long, poisonous projections.

Seahorse

If fish held dance competitions, the seahorse would win! Each day, seahorse couples greet each other with a beautiful dance. They swim in graceful swirls, circling each other as they move. The male and female seahorse also dance and swim with their tails linked. These stylish displays can last for just a few minutes or for hours.

The seahorse looks like no other fish. Its head has a long muzzle, which makes the fish resemble a horse.

The seahorse has a long mouth shaped like a tube. It uses it to suck in food.

The seahorse has bony plates in place of scales. The plates deter predators.

Top Talent

Seahorses are weak swimmers so they use their **prehensile** tail to grasp onto plants and **corals**. This stops the fish from being swept away by strong waves. The seahorse is camouflaged against rocks and plants by its colors, hiding it from predators.

Females do not carry baby seahorses. Instead, they develop inside a pouch on the male seahorse's stomach.

Great Dad

Seahorses dance as part of their **courtship**. At the end of the dance, the female places up to 2,000 eggs in a pouch on the male's stomach. The eggs attach to the pouch wall, through which they receive the oxygen and **nutrients** they need to develop until the baby seahorses inside hatch.

Sailfish

The sailfish is the fastest fish in the ocean and a swimming superstar! It can reach speeds of up to 68 miles (110 km) per hour. The fish is also a magnificent-looking creature. It is named for the spectacular sail fin on its back, which is almost as long as its body. The fin can stand upright, like a sail. The sailfish's upper jaw forms a long, spear-like bill.

The fish uses its long, sharp bill to stun and spear prey.

The fish's long, streamlined body and pointed bill are designed for speed.

Sails Up!

Sailfish usually keep their sails folded when they are swimming underwater. They raise their sail fin when they are swimming on the water's surface, or when they are threatened, to make themselves appear bigger. The fish also hunt in groups and use their sail fins to herd schools of sardines, squid, or anchovies to make them easier to catch.

The sailfish can grow to be more than 10 feet (3 m) long.

Secret Stars

Another super-fast swimmer is the shortfin mako shark. The shark can propel its torpedo-shaped body through the water at speeds of up to 31 miles (50 km) per hour. This shark is a menacing predator that locates tuna, dolphins, and other prey with its large black eyes. It slices through its prey with razor-sharp, knife-like teeth.

Archerfish

The archerfish is a super-accurate water shooter that hits its target every time! This talented fish shoots powerful jets of water from its mouth to knock its unsuspecting insect prey from plants that hang above the water. The insect then falls into the water, where the archerfish can eat it.

The archerfish can shoot accurately from up to 6 feet (2 m) away.

The archerfish has such an excellent aim that it can hit insects flying through the air.

Some types of archerfish can squirt several drops of water in a row, but others can fire only one shot at a time.

Secret Stars

In the swamp waters of Africa, the eel catfish feeds by sucking food into its mouth. To feed on insects on the muddy swamp shores, the fish can lift the front of its body out of the water to propel itself onto land. The fish then lunges at its prey and swallows it.

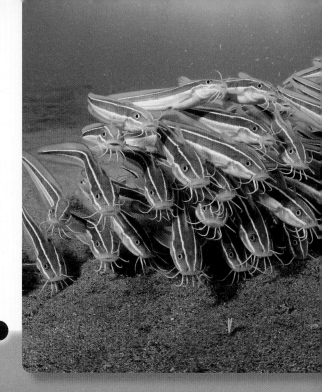

Gill Power!

How does the archerfish produce such a powerful jet of water? It presses its tongue against a groove in the roof of its mouth to form a tube shape. Then the fish squeezes its gill covers to force a stream of water through the tube and out of its mouth. The powerful stream of water can shoot more than 3 feet (90 cm) into the air.

The archerfish uses its gills to breathe but also to force water out of its mouth.

Gill

19

Flying Fish

This fish takes gold medal for the high jump! The flying fish can shoot out of the water at great speed and then glide through the air at heights of up to 12 feet (4 m) and for distances of up to 600 feet (180 m). The fish flies so high that it sometimes lands on the decks of ships!

The flying fish has a streamlined body that allows it to cut through air and water.

The flying fish has large, hard fins that can spread wide like a bird's wings.

Takeoff!

A flying fish glides rather than flies. It swims very fast toward the water's surface with its fins folded tightly against its body. Near the surface, it flaps its tail up and down to thrust itself out of the water. As it does so, the fish spreads its fins. Then, it glides a few feet (m) above the ocean at around 10 miles (16 km) per hour.

Flying fish can make several glides in a row.

Secret Stars

The blue marlin is one of the biggest and most beautiful fish in the world. Although it is heavy, it can jump high out of the water. This ocean giant can reach 14 feet (4.3 m) in length. The incredible fish has even been known to leap out of the ocean and onto fishing boats!

21

Stonefish

The stonefish is the most venomous fish in the world. The poison it contains could kill a human within just two hours! The fish uses the poison to protect itself from danger. When a bigger fish approaches and threatens the stonefish, it raises the poisonous spikes on its back. If the spines are touched, they immediately release a deadly dose of poison.

The stonefish is named for its rough, stone-like skin and mottled colors of red, brown, and gray.

4/2/14

The stonefish has 13 spikes on its back. They are all filled with deadly venom.

The stonefish often buries itself in sand to wait for its prey to pass by.

In Disguise

The stonefish is especially deadly because it is so well-camouflaged. Its colors and shape help it blend in with the rocks, coral, or sand on the seabed. Lying perfectly still for long periods of time so it does not attract attention, the fish looks just like a stone to passers by. When a small fish or shrimp comes close, the stonefish quickly seizes it.

Secret Stars

Although the lionfish has 18 venomous spikes, it is not quite as deadly as the stonefish. Unlike the stonefish, the lionfish does not hide. Instead, it uses its flamboyant stripes and large, feathery fins to warn any approaching predators that it will deliver a painful sting if attacked.

Electric Eel

This fish is truly shocking! It stuns its prey with one flick of its electrifying tail. The electric eel's body contains parts that store electrical power so it is always ready to strike. The eel can release a burst of electricity of up to 600 volts, a charge powerful enough to give a human a jolt. After stunning its prey, the eel sucks it into its mouth and straight into its stomach.

Despite its name, the fish is not an eel. It is more closely related to carp and catfish.

The fish has a long, thin body and a flat head. Its body is usually green or gray on top and yellow beneath.

The electric eel can grow to 9 feet (2.75 m) long and weighs up to 48.5 pounds (22 kg).

Power to Navigate

Electric eels live in murky pools and rivers in South America. The fish have poor eyesight so to find their way and locate prey, they emit a small electrical charge, which they use like a radar. They may also use their electric organs to communicate with other electric eels.

Electric eels use electric shocks to deter predators.

Secret Stars

One of the strangest-looking electric fish is the elephant fish. It is named for its long mouthpart, which looks a little like an elephant's trunk. The fish uses the mouthpart to feed on creatures in the mud of riverbeds. The fish has sensors in its nose that pick up weak electrical signals given off by prey. This allows the eel to find prey in muddy water.

Manta Ray

The manta ray is an incredibly elegant swimmer. When it moves through the water, it slowly flaps its enormous fins up and down, like wings. Despite its huge size, the manta ray feeds on some of the tiniest creatures in the ocean. It opens its mouth wide to filter huge amounts of **plankton** from the water as it swims along.

The manta ray's large, triangular side fins span up to 23 feet (7 m).

The paddle-like fins at the front of the ray's head form a funnel shape to channel plankton-rich water.

Top Talent

Mantas stay healthy by enlisting other fish to clean them. They let fish such as wrasse and remoras hitch a ride on their body. The fish then feed on the pieces of dead skin, **parasites**, and fallen food that collect on the rays' scales. Sometimes, manta rays even stop swimming above a group of remora fish, then wait patiently while the fish carry out their cleaning role!

Manta Magic

Not only does the manta ray swim beautifully, it also performs acrobatics. The ray has been seen jumping clear of the water, and splashing back down head or tail first. The manta ray also somersaults in the air with its fins spread wide. Experts believe the ray may do this to signal to other manta rays.

Amazing Adaptations

Some animals are superstars because they have developed special body features to help them survive. This is called physical **adaptation**. For example, the Antarctic icefish survives in freezing water because chemicals in its blood act like antifreeze to stop the fish from freezing.

The leafy sea dragon looks like the seaweed on which it lives. This hides the creature from any nearby predators.

Behavioral Adaptations

Some adaptations are behavioral. These are things that animals do to survive. For example, some rays bury themselves under the sand of the seabed and wait until prey passes. They then shoot out of the sand to catch the victim. Yellow saddle goatfish operate as a team to catch food. Their behavioral adaptations are one of the many features that make fish some of nature's superstars.

One saddle goatfish chases prey, while the others group together to block any escape routes.

Top Talent

Gills are adaptations that allow fish to breathe underwater. Gills contain many thin blood vessels. As water passes over the gills, oxygen that has dissolved in the water moves into the blood vessels and is then carried around the body.

29

Glossary

adaptation (a-dap-TAY-shun) A feature or way of behaving that helps an animal survive.

camouflage (KA-muh-flahj) The natural coloring or shape of an animal that allows it to blend in with its surroundings.

corals (KOR-ulz) Underwater organisms. The bodies of corals form coral reefs.

courtship (KORT-ship) The method by which a male and female animal attract each other.

fossil (FO-sul) The remains of an ancient animal.

gills (GILZ) Body parts that fish use for breathing.

invertebrates (in-VER-teh-brets) Animals that do not have backbones.

nutrients (NOO-tree-ents) The substances living things obtain from their food.

oxygen (OK-sih-jen) A gas that animals must breathe in order to survive.

parasites (PER-uh-sytz) Animals that live in or on another animal's body.

predator (PREH-duh-tur) An animal that hunts and eats other animals.

prehensile (pree-HEN-sul) Capable of grasping.

prey (PRAY) An animal that is hunted and eaten by other animals.

scales (SKAYLZ) Small, stiff, flat plates that overlap to form an outer covering on a fish's body.

toxin (TOK-sun) A poison.

vertebrates (VER-tih-brits) Animals that have backbones.

Further Reading

Hardyman, Robyn. *Fishing*. Adventures in the Great Outdoors. New York: Windmill Books, 2014.

Miller, Tori. *Sea Urchins*. Freaky Fish. New York: PowerKids Press, 2009.

Niver, Heather Moore. *20 Fun Facts About Lionfish*. Fun Fact File: Fierce Fish! New York: Gareth Stevens, 2013.

Websites

Due to the changing nature of Internet links, PowerKids Press has developed an online list of websites related to the subject of this book. This site is updated regularly. Please use this link to access the list:
www.powerkidslinks.com/ngt/fish/

Index